MW01697841

the full ARMOR OF GOD BIBLE STUDY

the full ARMOR OF GOD BIBLE STUDY

Darlene Schacht
The Time-Warp Wife

TIME-WARP WIFE
TIMEWARPWIFE.COM

Time-Warp Wife Ministries

All Scripture quotations, as indicated, are taken from the New International or the King James Version of the Bible

The Full Armor of God: Bible Study

Publisher:
Time-Warp Wife Ministries
25 Medinah Drive
Winnipeg, Manitoba
R0G 0A1

Cover design by Darlene Schacht
Interior design by Darlene Schacht

Images provided by Bigstock.com

ISBN 978-1-988984-10-0

Table of Contents

Ephesians 6:14-17

Stand therefore, having your loins girt about with truth, and having on the breastplate of righteousness; And your feet shod with the preparation of the gospel of peace; Above all, taking the shield of faith, wherewith ye shall be able to quench all the fiery darts of the wicked. And take the helmet of salvation, and the sword of the Spirit, which is the word of God.

The Helmet of Salvation

Let us be sober, putting on faith and love as a breastplate, and the hope of salvation as a helmet. (1 Thessalonians 5:8, NIV)

The Breastplate of Righteousness

Above all else, guard your heart, for everything you do flows from it. (Proverbs 4:23, NIV)

The Shield of Faith

Resist him, standing firm in the faith, because you know that the family of believers throughout the world is undergoing the same kind of sufferings. (1 Peter 5:9, NIV)

The Belt of Truth

Stand therefore, having your loins girt about with truth. (Ephesians 6:14a, KJV)

The Sword of the Spirit

For the word of God is alive and active. Sharper than any double-edged sword, it penetrates even to dividing soul and spirit, joints and marrow; it judges the thoughts and attitudes of the heart. (Hebrews 4:12, NIV)

Feet Shod With The Preparation of the Gospel of peace

And your feet shod with the preparation of the gospel of peace; (Ephesians 6:15)

CHAPTER 1

THE ENEMY

Regardless of how many times society tries to deny it, there's more to this world than that which we can see, touch, and hear. There's the physical realm and a spiritual realm. There's good and evil. There's a God at work in our lives and an enemy who seeks to destroy us.

> *The Bible tells us, "Be sober, be vigilant; because your adversary the devil, as a roaring lion, walketh about, seeking whom he may devour." (1 Peter 5:8, KJV)*

I wonder—how many of us are truly on guard? Are we prepared for an attack? Are we cautiously observing the way that we live, what we're listening to, and what we're allowing into our minds?

Last summer two dangerous fugitives were on the run in Canada. Newspaper headlines warned us that they were close to home. People were on the lookout. Keeping our ears and our eyes open, we kept watch. In fact, one small town in our province was instructed to stay in their homes until the impending danger was gone. We warned our children to be careful, did everything we could to protect them, and we ourselves were careful as well. That's how it should be when the enemy is approaching. We must be attentive, watchful, and wise.

In Old Testament times, towers were built so that watchmen could stand guard to look over the fields or the gates of a city. Because of its height one could see the enemy approaching from a distance, giving them enough time to sound a warning. He saw who came and who went through the city gates.

Ezekiel Chapter 33:1-6 lays out the duty of a watchman whose job it was to blow the horn as danger approached. The scripture also points out that those who hear the sound have a responsibility to heed the warning. I encourage you to study this beautiful portion of scripture, and to meditate on its words.

So, who is this lion the Bible is talking about? Who is the enemy we should be cautious of?

Ephesians 6:11 says, "Put on the whole armour of God, that ye may be able to stand against the wiles of the devil." The word "devil" that we see there is translated from the Greek word, "diabolos" (Strong's G1228) which means to slander or defame. Satan is also known as Lucifer, the accuser, the deceiver, the evil one, the wicked one, the destroyer, and the ruler of this world.

While the Bible clearly points out who Satan is and the danger he poses to us, most Americans (even those who refer to themselves as 'Christian') don't believe in the existence of Satan. In fact, a nation-wide survey conducted by The Barna Group revealed that 40% of Christians strongly agreed that Satan "is not a living being but is a symbol of evil. That tells us 40% are ignoring the fact that Jesus Himself said, "I saw Satan fall like lightning from heaven." (Luke 10:18, NIV)

The first step in defending ourselves against the enemy is acknowledging that he exists. If we don't believe there's an enemy, how could we possibly recognize the potential danger we're in?

We see Satan depicted in books, cartoons, and movies as a red-horned maniac wielding a pitchfork. The reality is, however, that he's not so easy to recognize as one might think. In fact, 2 Corinthians 11:14, Paul says that "he masquerades as an angel of light." He's a wolf in sheep's clothing, a lion concealed by the shadows, waiting to pounce.

The Struggle is Real

DID YOU KNOW

Satan is compared to a lion, and like a lion, he looks for easy prey; those who are alone, the young, or the wounded.

I've heard the saying "in like a lion and out like a lamb" in reference to the month of March. Year after year, the first week is ushered in by harsh weather, but by the 31st, we're greeted with warm temperatures and clear skies. On the flip side of that, Satan's character could be described as "in like a lamb and out like a lion." He comes to us ever so softly and unassuming, with cunning words and flattering lips he deceives. His sole agenda is to devour us by tearing us down. He wants to see both our lives and our spirits destroyed, and until he does that he'll revisit again and again.

> Satan is hungry and gullible ill-prepared Christians are on his menu.
> - Skip Heitzig -

Peter warns us. Like a watchman who's guarding the city he shouts from the tower, "Your enemy the devil prowls around like a roaring lion looking for someone to devour. Resist him," he says. "Stand firm in the faith."

The question is, what weapons do we have in our armory? What protection do we have against this impending attack?

Ephesians Chapter 6:10-18 answers this question loud and clear as Paul lays out the full armor of God. As I write this, I can't stress the word "full" enough, for every piece of armor from The Belt of Truth to The Sword of the Spirit is a vital part of our defence. We must be fully protected and empowered through the working of the Holy Spirit at all times.

That fight you had with your husband… that rift between family members… those doubts you had about your faith… the anger you felt when you were betrayed… that temptation that led you astray… the real enemy there was Satan and his army of angels.

Paul writes, "For our struggle is not against flesh and blood, but against the rulers, against the authorities, against the powers of this dark world and against the spiritual forces of evil in the heavenly realms. Therefore, put on the full armor of God, so that when the day of evil comes, you may be able to stand your ground, and after you have done everything, to stand." (Ephesians 6:12-13, NIV)

The Devil is vicious, but he's not victorious.
And you, my friend, have
everything you need to defeat him.
- Lysa Terkeurst -

Q. According to a survey conducted by the Barna Group, what percentage of people who refer to themselves as "Christian" believe Satan is just a symbol of evil, and not a living being?

____

____

____

____

Q. Which two realms are mentioned in this chapter?

____

____

____

____

____

____

DID YOU KNOW

Revelation 12:4 describes Satan as a red dragon who took one third of the stars of heaven (angels) with him when he fell.

Q. What does Revelation 12:4 say? Write the verse out here:

DID YOU KNOW

The horn the watchman blew was known as the Shofar? The Shofar is used repeatedly throughout the Bible including at the capture of Jericho when the walls fell, and the giving of the law on Mount Sinai.

Q. What does Satan masquerade as?

Q. Who is known as The Ruler of This World?

Q. What does James 4:7 teach us about handling temptation?

Q. Peter warns us about the dangers of Satan, but then reveals to us how we are to overcome him. What is Peter's advice to us?

What are the different names given or used to describe Satan in the Bible?

Job 1:6

Isaiah 14:12

Ezekiel 28:14

Matthew 4:1 ____________________

Matthew 4:3 ____________________

Matthew 9:34 ____________________

Matthew 12:24 ____________________

Matthew 13:39 ____________________

John 14:30 ____________________

2 Corinthians 4:4 ____________________

2 Corinthians 6:15 ____________________

Ephesians 2:2 ____________________

Revelation 9:11 ____________________

Revelation 12:9 ____________________

Revelation 12:10 ____________________

Stand
firm then,
with the belt of
truth buckled
around your
waist.
Ephesians 6:14

Chapter 2

The Belt of Truth

Before we begin to examine the first piece of armor, we must understand that we're not fighting this battle alone.

> *Paul writes, "Wherefore let him that thinketh he standeth take heed lest he fall." (1 Corinthians 10:12, KJV)*

The battle belongs to the Lord. He uses the small, the flawed, and the few to further the gospel, so that through our weakness His grace abounds all the more. A young shepherd boy slays a giant, not because he is mighty, but because God, working and moving within David, was bigger than any force on this earth. He pares down Gideon's army, before sending them off to battle, so that He might display His strength and His power. He leads an army to victory, through obedience to His Word in the battle of Jericho, so that all might see the supremacy of their God.

If we want to live in fullness of life, abounding with joy, we must be on guard to protect our hearts and our minds, ready to fight for what's rightfully ours. We need to fight for our families, our faith, our marriages, and in fact, we need to fight for our joy.

Stop and think about that for a minute. When was the last time you let Satan steal your joy? If you're married, when was the last time you let him get a foot hold in your marriage? Are you raising children? If so, are you getting down on your knees to fight for their soul? Are you defeating Satan or is he defeating you?

As we go through this study we'll examine the weapons of spiritual warfare. Weapons that cast down strong holds, destroy arguments, and demolish anything that threatens to stand in our way of living a victorious life in Christ.

Paul writes, "For though we live in the world, we do not wage war as the world does. The weapons we fight with are not the weapons of the world. On the contrary, they have divine power to demolish strongholds. We demolish arguments and every pretension that sets itself up against the knowledge of God, and we take captive every thought to make it obedient to Christ." (2 Corinthians 10:3–5)

Walk in this Truth

Looking to Ephesians 6:14a we find The Belt of Truth, "Stand therefore, having your loins girt about with truth." (KJV), you'll notice some other translations use the term, "gird our loins" with The Belt of Truth. This is an old saying that isn't used all that much anymore and in fact most of us haven't seen it used outside of the Bible. We do however see it used often throughout scripture. One example we find is in Exodus chapter 12 when the Lord instructed the Israelites to eat the Passover with their loins girded, their shoes on their feet and their staves in their hands.

The idea of girding your loins is to prepare yourself for battle, or in the case of the Passover they were preparing to eat and run at any moment. In ancient times, Roman soldiers wore tunics, which were masculine forms of a dress. The tunic was held snugly in place by a belt around the waist. The skirt was then lifted up and tucked into the belt so that one could move freely and swiftly. When you're out on the combat field, you don't want your tunic hindering your ability to defend yourself.

We see a similar idea in Hebrews 12:1 where it says, "Let us throw off everything that hinders and the sin that so easily entangles. And let us run with perseverance the race marked out for us." (NIV)

As we talk about truth in this chapter, let's be careful not to confuse it with The Sword of the Spirit. Of course, The Sword of the Spirit is a vital part of our armor, and we will get to that in a later chapter, but we must understand that there's a slight difference between the two in that one is *truth* while the other is *truthfulness*. One is knowing God's Word and the other is living a life of integrity.

DID YOU KNOW

Truth has been debated by a number of philosophers spanning several centuries. These debates resulted in many theories as to what truth is, including the modern idea of being true to oneself. In contrast, the noble Bereans searched the scriptures to find truth.

The original Greek word for truth in this context is *alētheia* (Strong's G225) which comes from the root word *alēthēs* (Strong's G227) which means "loving the truth, speaking the truth, truthful."

Truthfulness is not only knowing the truth, it's conforming to truth, and loving the truth. I remember a few years ago my son who was about 18 at the time, walked down to the bank to deposit his cheque. By the time he got there, it was getting dark. The parking lot was empty and there wasn't sole in sight, when he happened upon 160 dollars laying on the ground. Eight crisp 20 dollar bills were lying on the pavement waiting to be scooped up and spent. My son picked up the money alright, but then he sat down on the curb, took out his phone and called me.

"Mom," he said. "I'll be a while. I found money on the ground, and I want to hang around here a while just in case someone comes looking for it."

No one did. No one saw him pick it up, and no one came looking for it. Because he loves truth, however, he went to the bank the next day and turned in the money. That's integrity. It's found in those quiet moments when no one but God sees the work of your hands.

God's plan for you is to move you into a position of impact by infusing you with truth and employing you with prayer.
- Priscilla Shirer -

Authentic truthfulness is more than doing the right thing, it's a deep-rooted *desire* to do the right thing. It's the difference between generous hands that everyone sees and a generous heart that's hidden with God.

Hebrews 4:13 says, "Nothing in all creation is hidden from God's sight. Everything is uncovered and laid bare before the eyes of him to whom we must give account." (NIV)

If you're not loving truth and walking in truth, you're going to cave the moment you're tempted—and you will be tempted I can promise you that.

Satan likes to isolate us before he attacks because he knows that our actions don't always match up with our hearts. He knows that its best to attack when we're not seeking praise and approval. (Remember, Jesus was led into the wilderness by the Spirit to be tempted by Satan). You know as well as I do that we're more likely to fall when we're not being watched. But integrity isn't integrity at all if we don't practice in secret that which we hold dear in the light.

You lose your strength
dear Christian, the moment you
depart from your integrity.
- Charles H. Spurgeon -

In Philippians 1:10 Paul writes, "That ye may approve things that are excellent; that ye may be sincere and without offence till the day of Christ." The word he uses for sincerity is the same word Peter uses in 2 Peter 3:1 translated as, "pure minds." (KJV) This word, *elikrinēs* (Strong's G1506) is defined as: found pure when unfolded and examined by the sun's light.

In his commentary on Philippians, James Montgomery Boice writes, "In ancient times the biggest industry in the world was the pottery industry. And pottery varied in quality just as cars, office supplies, or household goods vary today. The cheapest pottery was thick and solid and did not require much skill to make. It is found everywhere at archaeological sites. The finest pottery was thin. It had a clear color, and it brought a high price. Fine pottery was very fragile both before and after firing, and it would often crack in the oven. Cracked pottery should have been thrown away. But dishonest dealers were in the habit of filling in the cracks with a hard pearly wax that would blend in with the color of the pottery. This made the cracks practically undetectable in the shops, especially when painted or glazed; but the wax was immediately detectable when the pottery was held up to light, especially the sun. It was said that the artificial element was detected by "sun-testing." Honest dealers marked their finer product by the caption sine cera—'without wax.'"

And so, Paul tells us to arm ourselves with The Belt of Truth. Walk in truthfulness. Cast off anything that hinders you, turn away from any sin that entangles you, and get ready to fight.

Rather, we have renounced secret and shameful ways; we do not use deception, nor do we distort the word of God. On the contrary, by setting forth the truth plainly we commend ourselves to everyone's conscience in the sight of God. (2 Corinthians 4:2, NIV)

Q. According to the writer of the book of Hebrews, what are we to run with?

Q. What is the meaning of "Sine Cera?"

DID YOU KNOW

Just hours before His crucifixion, Jesus appeared before Pilate and was expected to give a defense of the charges against Him. Instead, He used this time to speak of truth. This surprised Pilate and prompted his response, "what is truth?"

Q. What is the meaning of the phrase "gird your loins?"

Q. Where did the Holy Spirit lead Jesus to be tempted?
In what 3 ways was Jesus tempted?

Q. If we want to live in fullness of life, abounding with joy, what must we protect?

DID YOU KNOW

The only breed of dog mentioned by name in the Bible is the greyhound (Proverbs 30:29-31, KJV). The Hebrew phrase translated as "greyhound" literally means "girt in the loins." This probably was considered by translators the most appropriate English term to describe the ancestor of the greyhound.

Q. According to Hebrews 12:1, what is it that can so easily entangle us? And so, what are we to do?

Q. When does a person's integrity become hypocrisy?

FOOD FOR THOUGHT

When Jesus takes the wheel, He takes us on a journey through rough terrain and barren land. He leads us to and through the heart of a storm before He safely drives us out.

Why? Because one will never be complete without the trying of our faith. And so, we experience sickness and death, poverty and sorrow and pain.

As gold refined in a fire, so is the trying of our faith.

Charles Spurgeon once said, "Whenever God means to make a man great, He always breaks him in pieces first."

We see this throughout scripture as men and women are brought down to their knees before they are lifted back up. Joseph is sold into slavery by his brothers. David is relentlessly chased down by King Saul, and then later betrayed by his son. Moses is led through the desert of testing for 40 years. Paul is beaten, tortured, imprisoned, and blind, all for the sake of the gospel.

At the center of each one of their lives, there's one thing that stands out more than anything else. One thing sets them apart from the others. One thing shines bright: it's the simple fact that they lived in obedience to their faith.

6 Ways to Stay Faithful

PRAY

Watch and pray so that you will not fall into temptation. The spirit is willing, but the flesh is weak. (Matthew 26:41, NIV)

Be Strong

Finally, be strong in the Lord and in his mighty power. Put on the full armor of God, so that you can take your stand against the devil's schemes. (Ephesians 6:10-11, NIV)

Resist

Submit yourselves, then, to God. Resist the devil, and he will flee from you. (James 4:7, NIV)

Study

I have hidden your word in my heart that I might not sin against you. (Psalm 119:11, NIV)

Stay Alert

Be alert and of sober mind. Your enemy the devil prowls around like a roaring lion looking for someone to devour. (1 Peter 5:8, NIV)

OBEY

How can a young person stay on the path of purity? By living according to your word. (Psalm 119:9, NIV)

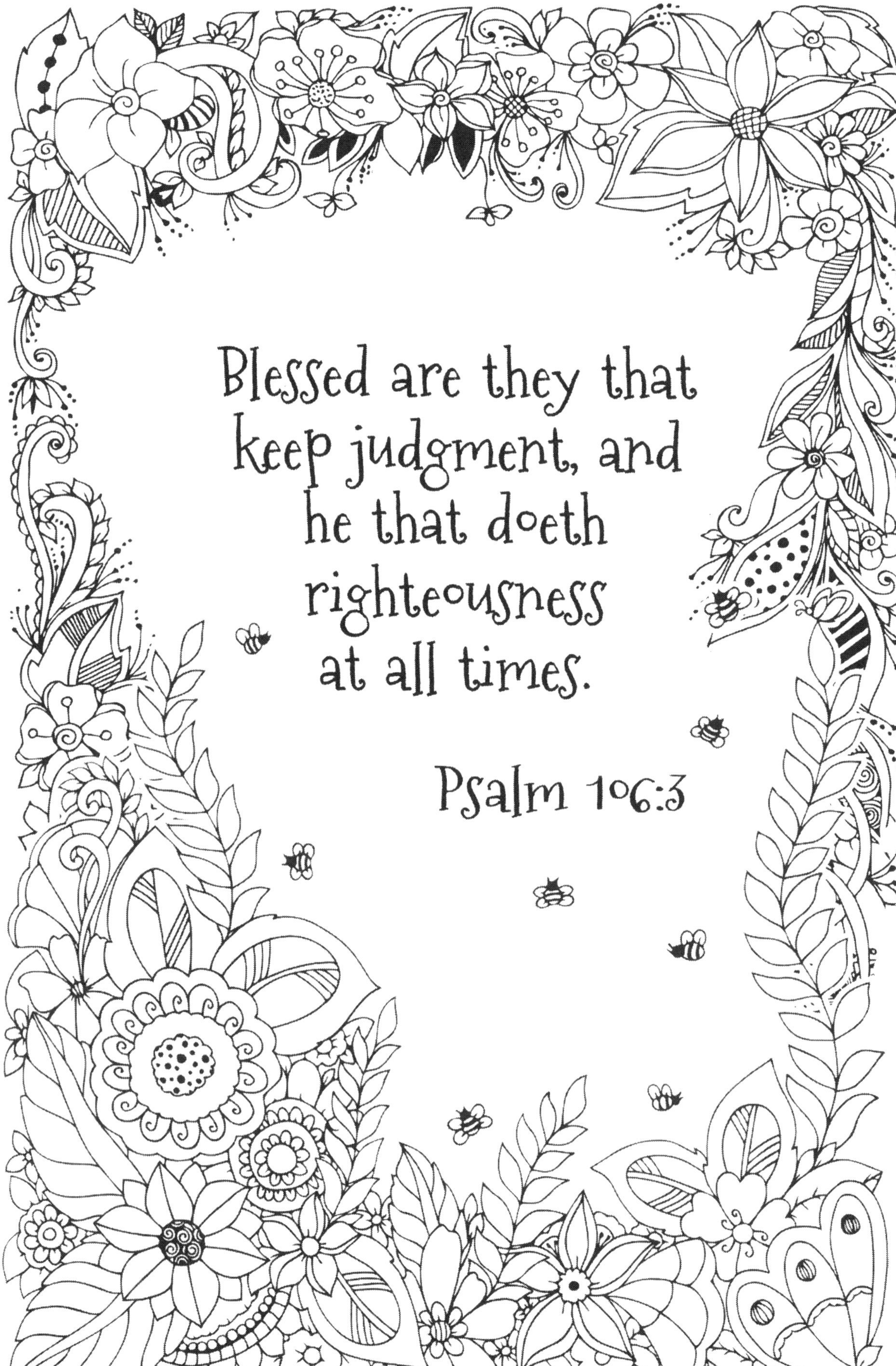

Blessed are they that
keep judgment, and
he that doeth
righteousness
at all times.

Psalm 106:3

Chapter 3

The Breastplate of Righteousness

I received a message from a friend a few years back. She was about to step into women's ministry, and definitely felt God nudging her in this direction. She was everything you want someone in ministry to be—excited, prepared, and ready to be used by the Lord. But here's the thing: someone told her she wasn't good enough, and she believed it. Hearing those words coming from the mouth of one of her peers was a swift kick to the gut.

She allowed Satan to steal her joy, deflate her sense of self-worth and question her calling. He's the master manipulator of half-truths, who comes to kill, steal, and destroy. You see, on one hand it was true. She wasn't good enough. But the thing is, none of us are. Not one. She's not good enough, I'm not good enough, even Billy Graham wasn't good enough. But here's the thing our righteousness comes through faith in Jesus Christ, and He is more than good enough. Throughout history He's used people that were weak and small and flawed to further the gospel. He's using cracked vessels for His glory and honor, so that through our weakness His grace abounds all the more.

In Isaiah 64:6, the Bible describes the righteous acts of the unbelievers as filthy rags. What the writer was referring to here when he wrote "filthy rags" were actually menstruation cloths that were used, washed, and hung out on the fence to dry. They'd shrivel up, fade, and sometimes even blow away in the wind.

But we are all as an unclean thing, and all our righteousnesses are as filthy rags; and we all do fade as a leaf; and our iniquities, like the wind, have taken us away. (Isaiah 64:6)

It's gross, but that's exactly the point the author of Isaiah was trying to make. We're deceiving ourselves if we think we are something without the righteousness of Christ.

God made him who had no sin to be sin for us, so that in him we might become the righteousness of God. (2 Corinthians 5:21)

And be found in him, not having mine own righteousness, which is of the law, but that which is through the faith of Christ, the righteousness which is of God by faith. (Philippians 3:9, KJV)

The righteousness we're talking about here, is a gift that's imputed to us. It's a right standing with God through faith in Jesus Christ. It's given to us by grace, and there's nothing we can do to earn it. But there's another righteousness I want to talk about in this chapter, and that's the righteousness we're commanded to live by. The difference here is that one is a gift and the other is our responsibility.

To put on The Breastplate of Righteousness is to live a righteous life. It's something we put on every day. Don't get me wrong— The Breastplate of Righteousness is not self-righteousness—it's our response to the righteousness imputed by Christ. As Paul writes, "I press on to take hold of that for which Christ Jesus took hold of me."

We won't be perfect, but we can and should be progressive. Progress is development and improvement. It's movement toward a goal. Just as a baby grows within the womb so we must develop and progress as we're growing in Christ.

If you look at images of Roman breastplates, you'll see they take on a vest-like shape, and were generally made of leather, bronze, or iron. The breastplate was worn over the tunic, and served to protect the vital organs within the upper torso.

Protect Your Heart

The Breastplate of Righteousness serves to protect the heart. In fact, Proverbs 4:23 tells us, "Above all else, guard your heart, for everything you do flows from it." Every choice we make, and every action we take stems from the heart. Our priorities, our convictions, our ideas, and our belief systems are all formed in the heart.

DID YOU KNOW

In Romans 2:7, Paul sums up righteousness as "perseverance in doing good," and unrighteousness as being selfishly ambitious and disobedient to the truth.

If everything we do flows from the heart, then we must do our best to protect our hearts by guarding our thoughts and filling our minds with the truth of God's word.

DID YOU KNOW

The bullet-proof vest is a modern descendant of the ancient breastplate.

In 2 Corinthians 10:5, Paul writes, "We demolish arguments and every pretension that sets itself up against the knowledge of God, and we take captive every thought to make it obedient to Christ."

The words he uses here are likened to warfare. We see the crumbling walls of a fortress as enemy soldiers are brought to their knees.

DID YOU KNOW

Job protected his heart by making a covenant with his eyes, that he would not look upon a young woman with lust.(Job 31:1)

In one of his sermons, Charles Spurgeon shared a parable of a Dervish man from the East who came upon a mountain. Looking down from the mountain, he saw the sun shining brightly on a river stream. It looked beautiful from afar, but as the old man made his way down the mountain, he soon discovered that this river was muddy and unfit for drinking.

Nearby, he saw a young shepherd boy busy filtering water. With much effort and time, he sifted and filtered the muddy water each day for his flock. Little by little he purified the water, collecting it in a cistern so the animals might have clean water to drink.

Knowing that there was a better way, the Dervish man instructed the young shepherd to follow him. For miles they journeyed through rough terrain until they came to the source of the stream. Just as they arrived a flock of birds flew away while wild beasts rushed into the forest. They found an open well that was continually flowing, but the beasts that came to drink had perpetually disturbed the soil around it. Because of these animals the well was turbid and muddy.

"My son," said the wise man. "Set to work now to protect the fountain and guard the well, which is the source of this stream. If you can keep these wild beasts and fouls away, the stream will flow pure and clear."

And so, while the young man went to work guarding the stream, the old man said, "My son if thou art wrong, seek not to correct thine outward life, but first seek to get thy heart correct. For out of it are the issues of life, and thy life shall be pure once thy heart is so."

Q. What are Paul's words in 2 Corinthians 10:5 likened to?

Q. What were Roman breastplates made of?

Righteousness

Q. What does it mean to put on The Breastplate of Righteousness?

Q. What does Proverbs 4:23 tell us to guard? Write the verse out here.

Q. What are some practical ways you can protect your heart?

Fill in the Blanks:

If you know that he is ________________, you know that everyone who does ________________ has been born of him. (1 John 2:29, NIV)

For with the heart man believeth unto ________________; and with the mouth confession is made ________________. (Romans 10:10, KJV)

All Scripture is God-breathed and is useful for teaching, rebuking, correcting and ____________________________, so that the servant of God may be thoroughly ________________ for every good work. (2 Timothy 3:16-17, NIV)

Q. With what are we to fill our minds?

Q. What does Paul say we should take captive? How do we do that?

Not that I have already obtained all this, or have already arrived at my goal, but I press on to take hold of that for which Christ Jesus took hold of me.

Philippians 3:12, NIV

Q. What are some reoccurring thoughts that you struggle to take captive?
What are some enticing lies that Satan has told you about these thoughts?

What are some truths that can tear these lies down?

Be on your guard; stand firm in the faith; be courageous; be strong.

1 Cor. 16:13, NIV

Chapter 4

Feet Shod with the Gospel of Peace

Last year I completed the couch to 5k. Let me tell you, it wasn't easy. Not just because of my age, but mostly because I hadn't run for 10 years. I was so out of shape that the initial 30 seconds took everything I had just to push through. I didn't think I'd ever be able to do it, but somehow, I did.

A lot of persistence and a good pair of shoes go a long way when you're running a race. In fact, when I was looking for a good couch to 5k program, I couldn't help but notice that nearly every website I went to advised me to start with good shoes. Of course, I didn't listen at first, but that quickly changed when I realized the difference good footwear can make.

Footwear is designed with a purpose in mind. You don't wear snow shoes to the beach, and you wouldn't wear sandals in the snow. The same goes for a soldier preparing for battle. Combat boots are specifically designed to provide protection and stability. They're strong and sturdy and yet they're flexible enough for rugged terrain. They've got to be made of waterproof leather if they hope to withstand water and rocks.

In ancient times, Roman soldiers wore leather sandals known as "caligae." Caligae were heavy-duty sandals with hobnailed soles. The hobnails were hammered into the soles of the sandals to offer the soldiers extra grip much like the modern-day cleats worn by football players. In *Wars 6.1.8* Josephus, the Jewish Historian, writes, "... as Julian had shoes all full of thick and sharp nails as had every one of the other soldiers (caligae—cleats on the soles of shoes), so when he ran on the (smooth marble) floors of the temple, he slipped and fell down upon his back with a very great noise, which was made by his armor…"

DID YOU KNOW

Caliga (leather sandals) comes from the Latin word "callus" meaning hard. It's the same word we use to describe hard or thickened skin.

Likewise, soldiers of faith must be ready for combat with the right pair of shoes. The right pair of shoes in this case is the gospel of peace. What better shoes could we ever hope to receive than that which is made by the Master. A gospel of peace. A beautiful gospel that brings the good news of God to the sinner. Your sins are forgiven. Your time of freedom has come. Man has been reconciled to God through His Son.

The Bible tells us to stand firm with our feet shod with the preparation of the gospel of peace. The apostle Paul is telling us here to stand firm in our faith. Stand firm in the face of affliction. Don't waiver when you're tested and tried. Don't run when you're standing alone. Don't give up when the going is tough. Stand firm in the gospel of peace.

When you're feeling doubtful, give glory to God. When you're feeling afraid, give glory to God. When you're feeling discouraged give glory to God. Don't let your circumstances dictate the strength of your faith.

Acts Chapter 16 is a powerful lesson in faith. We see Paul and Silas stripped, severely beaten, and thrown into prison. But here's the interesting part in all this: Verse 25 tells us that around midnight, Paul and Silas were singing hymns and praying to God.

I stop at that verse in absolute awe of those men, and I realize they had something wonderful that the other prisoners didn't. They knew there was more to this life than the pain they were facing. They had faith in the gospel of peace.

Faith tells us that that eternal glory outweighs our momentary affliction by far. It reminds us that we have a home beyond the scope of this world, and points us straight to the salvation of God. Faith tells us to take our eyes off our problems today and to focus on the hope set before us.

Isaiah reminds us of the strength that comes to those who trust in the Lord as he writes,

Stand Firm in Faith

But they that wait upon the Lord shall renew their strength; they shall mount up with wings as eagles; they shall run, and not be weary; and they shall walk, and not faint. (Isaiah 40:31, KJV)

We can learn from eagles when it comes to our trials, or more particularly when it comes to rising above them. Unlike humans, eagles can sense when a storm is approaching. Not only are they ready for it—they set their wings in such a way that they are lifted by the wind. They soar above while the storm rages below them.

To have our feet shod with the gospel of peace is to stand firm in our faith. It's truly knowing what we know. You can't defend something if you're still wavering on it. James 1:8 says, "A double minded man is unstable in all his ways."

Here's the thing: when we truly know what we know, we're ready to defend what we know. In the same way, when we're armed with scripture we can draw from our faith. That's why the Bible tells us that the Word of God is sharper than any two-edged sword. It cuts through the lies that attack us and threaten to draw us away from the Lord.

We hear lies daily. Whether they're internal or external, Satan is doing his best to drag us down. His mission is to discourage us and draw us away from our faith. His tactics have a way of sucking the joy out of us until all that we're left with is a feeling of self-doubt and defeat.

Just knowing this makes me want to grab hold of scripture tighter than I ever have. I want to be like Jesus Who, while He was tempted, rebuked Satan's lies with the truth of God's Word. Why? Because He knew what He knew and was therefore ready to stand.

If you're not strong in your faith, you won't be strong in the fight. The Bible tells us that we're overcomers because of the power within us. We don't have to fight this battle alone. And we're not expected to fight this battle alone. We're merely vessels of His power and strength.

You, dear children, are from God and have overcome them, because the one who is in you is greater than the one who is in the world. (1 John 4:4, NIV)

Standing firm in the armor of
God doesn't stop the spiritual warfare from
raging. It stops it from defeating you.
- Tony Evans -

Q. What were the sandals Roman soldiers wore made of?

Q. Who were singing hymns and praying in prison in the middle of the night?

And from this peace those
sandals are prepared with which a man
may tread on the lion and the adder, yes,
and on the fierce burning coals of malice,
slander and persecution! What better
shoes can our souls require?
- Charles H. Spurgeon -

Strengthened by Adversity

Adversity does one of two things. It either knocks us off our feet and leaves us feeling defeated, or we are strengthened by it. Let's look at 9 people (and one nation) who were strengthened by the winds of adversity:

- Joseph was thrown into a pit and sold into slavery.
- The Hebrews were enslaved for hundreds of years by the Egyptians.
- Pharaoh tried to kill Moses more than once.
- Samson was weak, humiliated, blind, and in bondage.
- Job lost everything including his children.
- God wrestled with Jacob and put his thigh out of joint before he called him, "Israel" (who prevails with God).
- Ruth lost her husband. She left behind her home, and her people.
- David was a murderer, and an adulterer. He lost his infant son.
- Peter denied Christ three times on the night of His death.
- Paul was stricken with blindness for 3 days.

Q. How do we rebuke Satan's lies?

Q. List some of the trials you have experienced in your life. After each one, mark down whether you think you were strengthened or defeated by it:

Q. What outweighs our momentary affliction?

Q. What does God promise to those who wait upon the Lord?

Q. How did Josephus describe the soles of the Roman soldiers' shoes?

____

____

____

____

____

____

Fill in the Blanks:

Therefore, my dear brothers and sisters,
_______________________. Let nothing move you.
Always give yourselves fully to the work of the Lord,
because you know that your labor in the Lord is not
_______________________.
(1 Corinthians 15:58, NIV)

Q. How do we stand firm in our faith?

Q. When was the last time you let Satan steal your joy? What happened? How should you have reacted instead?

Notes

WE WAIT IN HOPE
FOR THE LORD;
HE IS OUR HELP
AND OUR SHIELD.
PSALM 33:20

CHAPTER 5

THE SHIELD OF FAITH

In Ephesians 6:16, Paul tells us to take up The Shield of Faith. What's interesting to note is that the original Greek word for "shield" here is thereos (Strong's #2375). It comes from the root word thyra which means a door. The large oblong four-cornered shield was given the name "thyreos" because of its resemblance to a door. Typically, these shields were made of a light-weight wood and covered with leather. The Romans used a similar shield (though it was concave) in ancient warfare known as the Great Scuta, and although they haven't been in use since around 300 AD, there is still one in existence at the Yale University Art Gallery.

These shields differed in design from the circular shields known at the time as the aspis. While the aspis was easier to carry and maneuver during combat, it couldn't provide the same protection that the thyreos could. With thereos in hand, soldiers were able to stand shoulder to shoulder forming a wall of protection. 2nd, 3rd, and 4th row soldiers formed a roof of protection by holding their shields overhead. This protected the army from flaming arrows both in front of them and from above. Search "thyreos formation" on Google Images and you'll see what I'm talking about.

DID YOU KNOW

The small round shield known as an Apsis was used primarily by soldiers on horseback.

Note that Paul writes "above all that," or "in addition to all that," take up The Shield of Faith. We're already being protected by other pieces of armor, but he's stressing the importance here of extra protection.

I remember back about 20 years ago to when my brother-in-law won $25,000 dollars in a scratch and win lottery. It wasn't enough for him to keep the ticket locked in the house for the night, he put it under his pillow for an extra layer of protection. He had to ensure that ticket was safe.

I remember buckling my babies into the car when they were young. I didn't just buckle them into their car seat, I made sure that the car seat was in the centre for that extra layer of protection.

DID YOU KNOW

The shields included a metal dome protruding from the middle of the shield (known as the "boss") which was used to knock the enemy off balance during battle.

If faith in Christ is our most valuable asset, shouldn't we also go to great lengths to protect it? Paul is telling us here to put on that extra layer of protection to shield ourselves from the flaming arrows of the evil one.

In ancient warfare, the Romans fastened pitch-soaked rags to their arrows with wire. These flammable rags were then lit on fire and launched at enemy lines. In order to quench those darts, the shields were saturated in water before going to battle.

So, what are these fiery darts that Satan is launching? What exactly are we shielding ourselves from?

John MacArthur points out that "The heart of all sin is dissatisfaction." In other words, the less we are satisfied, the more we'll be tempted. And so, we lust after power, money, attention, love, food, sex, beauty, and more. The thing is however, if we're not content with the things that we have, we won't be content if we're given more. Satan knows that dissatisfaction is the Achilles' heel of mankind. He knows that we hunger for more and so we're met with temptation day after day.

We're all born with a God-shaped hole inside of us that's waiting to be filled. Some people are filling that space with money and power and lust, but those who fill it with Christ are the ones who are most content in this world.

You can't expect to stay on a diet if you're spending most of your time in the bakery section of a supermarket. It's hard to resist the charms of a married co-worker if you're dating each other at lunch. In other words, if you don't want to be tempted, don't invite temptation for lunch. Don't open the door, or it will move in and take over your home.

These darts are the arguments that we entertain. The ones that justify our sin, and tempt us to step in further yet. These are the arrows that distort the truth of God's word, and reshape it into something it's not. But if we're truly immersed in God's Word, we know the truth from a lie. This is often referred to in scripture as the knowledge of the truth.

Arrows can travel well over 1,000 feet, but here's the interesting thing to remember. The farther the enemy is from the target the less powerful the arrows will be. In other words, the further we are from temptation, the less powerful Satan will be.

Here's a practical example of that. During our first few years of marriage, my husband and I were clueless when it came to our credit. We were easily drawn in by the "Don't Pay a Cent Event" slogans, and like a lot of young couples we misused our credit card any chance that we had. Thankfully our credit limit wasn't high enough to get us into any serious trouble, but it was high enough to give us a scare as we quickly reached our credit limit.

One Saturday afternoon, we came to the mutual conclusion to freeze our credit. Literally. Filling a small plastic bowl full of water, we froze the credit card into a solid block of ice. Our reasoning behind this was that if we really needed to access the credit card it would be there, but we'd have to wait for the ice to melt. In other words, it wouldn't be nearly as accessible as it was before. This separation from temptation was exactly what we needed to get back on track.

Separation from temptation goes a long way in protecting our hearts, but it's not our only means of protection. Anytime that we're angry or fearful or left wanting more, we can look to His Word to find hope.

Shield Yourself

These darts can also come in the form of discouraging lies. He'll tell you you're ugly, that you're a bad mom, that God doesn't care, that you have no friends, that you're not smart, and the list will go on...

DID YOU KNOW

Flaming arrows could only be used at relatively close distances. Shooting an arrow over a long distance would usually extinguish the flame.

There's joy to be found in our faith when we trust in the wisdom of God. There's incomparable peace to found in those pages. Words that remind us this world's not our home. A Savior who tells us that He's coming back. Love that sent our Lord to the cross so that we might be saved. Joy, peace, love, and hope—these are the faith-building blocks that we glean from God's Word. These are the things that fill the God-shaped hole that's within us.

DID YOU KNOW

The word "peace" is defined as "wholeness." Peace is living in the truth of the gospel.

Faith comes by hearing and hearing by the word of God. And so, we must be immersed in His Word as we fight the good fight. Like a soldier who immerses his shield in the river before going to battle, we too must be immersed by the cleansing power of His Word.

The Bible tells us, "Resist him, standing firm in the faith, because you know that the family of believers throughout the world is undergoing the same kind of sufferings." (1 Peter 5:9, NIV)

Q. What are the fiery darts spoken of in Ephesians Chapter 6?

The devil can handle me
but he can't handle the one to
whom I am joined.
- A. W. Tozer -

Q. How are the shields made
fire-proof?

Q. From where does faith originate?

Q. Why is dissatisfaction so dangerous to a believer?

Only a strong faith—a faith based on God's Word—will protect us from temptation and doubt.

- Billy Graham -

Q. What are the faith building blocks we glean from God's word?

Q. What has cleansing power?

____

____

Fill in the Blanks:

No ____________________ that is formed against thee shall prosper; and every tongue that shall rise against thee in judgment thou shalt condemn. This is the heritage of the servants of the LORD, and their ____________________ is of me, saith the LORD. (Isaiah 54:17, KJV)

Be ________________ and ____________________. Do not be afraid or terrified because of them, for the Lord your God goes with you; he will never leave you nor forsake you. (Deuteronomy 31:6, NIV)

But you, Lord, are _______________________ around me, my glory, the One who lifts my head high. (Psalm 3:3, NIV)

Q. What are some of the lies that Satan has been firing at you?
Under each one, mark down a fire-quenching truth.

Notes

Therefore, with minds that are alert and fully sober, set your hope on the grace to be brought to you when Jesus Christ is revealed at his coming.
1 Peter 1:13, NIV

Chapter 6

The Helmet of Salvation

If you've ever wondered what The Helmet of Salvation is, look at the verse from Paul's letter to the Thessalonian church where he defines it as hope:

> *But since we belong to the day, let us be sober, putting on faith and love as a breastplate, and the hope of salvation as a helmet. (1 Thessalonians 5:8, NIV)*

I can't imagine living in this world without hope. How could we possibly get through the pain of suffering and the agony of loss without the hope of something beyond the scope of this world?

Jesus says, *"I've gone to prepare a place for you..."* Those are the words I hold on to. Those are the words that remind me that this world isn't my home. That is the hope that I cling to when everything else is slipping away. He goes on to say, *"And if I go and prepare a place for you, I will come back and take you to be with me that you also may be where I am." (John 14:3, NIV)*

This hope of salvation took on an entirely deeper meaning for believers when Jesus died on the cross and rose from the dead. Paving the way, He was the first of many to follow. We don't serve a God Who merely *offers hope*, we serve a God Who is *the living hope* for all who believe.

In Leviticus 23:42-43, we read about the annual Feast of Tabernacles, where the Israelites were instructed to live in temporary shelters for seven days. These temporary dwellings were a physical reminder to them of what their ancestors had to live in for over 40 years as they wandered through the desert on their way to the promised land. It's also a physical reminder to us that this world is nothing more than a temporary dwelling as we wait for the return of our Lord.

In Matthew Chapter 17, we see Jesus taking Peter, James, and John up the top of a mountain. Suddenly, He's transfigured before them. Shining as bright as a light, He is standing with Moses and Elijah. Note that in Verse 4, Peter offers to build them each a shelter. See the connection here? It was the feast of tabernacles, a time for Jesus to illustrate the hope of salvation.

Jesus shone in His glorified body before them--a glimpse of His resurrection and power. But why Moses and Elijah? What was the significance of them being there with Jesus that day? The three were a representation of the coming kingdom in all of its glory. Moses represented believers who enter the kingdom through death. Elijah, a prophet who never saw death but was taken up to heaven in a whirlwind, represents believers who enter the kingdom through the rapture of the church. And let's not forget the fourth one that was with them that day--the voice of the Father exalting His Son.

The placement of this portion of scripture is vital. It immediately follows the words of Jesus telling them that He would not only die, but that He would return again with the angels in all of His glory.

I remember the year that my dad found out he had cancer. Most importantly I remember the joy and the peace that he had as he walked around the house singing,

Because He lives, I can face tomorrow
Because He lives, all fear is gone
Because I know He holds the future
And life is worth a living just because He lives

(William and Gloria Gaither, Capitol Christian Music Group)

In other words, there's a reason I can face tomorrow, there's a reason that my fear is gone, and there's a reason that life is worth living. That reason is the hope of salvation that comes through faith in Jesus Christ.

In 2 Peter Chapter 1, Peter points out how our faith isn't based on fables or clever stories, but on eye-witness accounts. He was there to witness the majesty of Jesus that day on the mountain and to hear the voice of the Father proclaim Christ as His Son.

In the same chapter, Peter refers to his body as a tent that he would be putting aside when he departed this earth. And so, we see this message throughout the Old Testament, and into the New—the temporary dwelling of the tabernacle or tent, in which our spirit resides, but more importantly, a hope of salvation through Christ. Without that hope of salvation, nothing makes sense.

In 2005, The National Science Foundation published an article in regard to human thought. According to the article, research indicated that 80% of our thoughts are negative and 95% are the same repetitive thoughts as the day before.

This negative pattern of thinking tells me that we need to be pro-active when it comes to protecting our minds. When Satan attacks he aims for the head. He plants thoughts in our minds designed to discourage, depress, and cause doubt. Isn't that the tactic he's used from the beginning of time? Appealing to Eve's hunger for knowledge and wisdom, the serpent succeeded in drawing her in.

Anyone who's been on a diet knows the pain of exchanging the long-term benefits that come with staying the course for a temporary high. And yet, in a sense that's what we're doing when we choose to follow our lust at the cost of our faith. We're choosing to cling to a world that is wasting away instead of the hope set before us.

What's interesting to note however, is that there's a benefit to our suffering. It produces endurance. If you've ever seen a strong person it's likely that they've been through a lot in their life, and it was those obstacles that produced perseverance. Perseverance in turn proves the validity of our character. If you are truly a servant of God you will continue to be faithful to God, and that faithfulness is the very thing that builds hope.

And we boast in the hope of the glory of God. Not only so, but we also glory in our sufferings, because we know that suffering produces perseverance; perseverance, character; and character, hope. (Romans 5:2b–4, NIV)

DID YOU KNOW

Did you know that the Greek word used in Romans 5:4
for character is "dokimē" which means
"approved tried character."

Well, That's Interesting

In the ancient world there was no banking system as we know it today, and no paper money. All money was made from metal, heated until liquid, poured into moulds and allowed to cool. When the coins were cooled, it was necessary to smooth off the uneven edges. The coins were comparatively soft, and of course many people shaved them closely. In one century, more than eighty laws were passed in Athens to stop the practice of whittling down the coins then in circulation. But some money-changers were men of integrity, who would accept no counterfeit money; they were men of honour who put only genuine, full-weight money into circulation. Such men were called dokimos [from the same word as dokimē], and this word is used here for the Christian as he is to be seen by the world.

(Donald Grey Barnhouse, Romans: God's Glory, p. 18)

Q. What are some long-term goals that you've had?
What are some of the short-term benefits that either slowed
you down or presented them from happening?

The helmet of salvation is that great hope of final salvation that gives us confidence and assurance that our present struggle with Satan will not last forever and we will be victorious in the end
- John MacArthur -

Fill in the Blanks:

For in this hope we ________________________. But hope that is seen is no hope at all. Who hopes for what they already have? But if we hope for what we do not ________________________, we wait for it ________________________.

(Romans 8:24-25, NIV)

If only for this life we have ________________ in Christ, we are of all people most to be __________________. (1 Corinthians 15:19, NIV)

In his great mercy he has given us new birth into a __________________ __________________ through the resurrection of Jesus Christ from the dead.

(1 Peter 1:3b)

Q. What two things are the temporary shelters found in Leviticus 23:42-43 a physical reminder of?

Q. What is the Helmet of Salvation according to 1 Thessalonians 5:8?

Q. What happened on the mountain in Matthew Chapter 17? Who was there with Jesus?

Q. What did Moses and Elijah each represent at the transfiguration?
What connection would this have to The Helmet of Salvation?

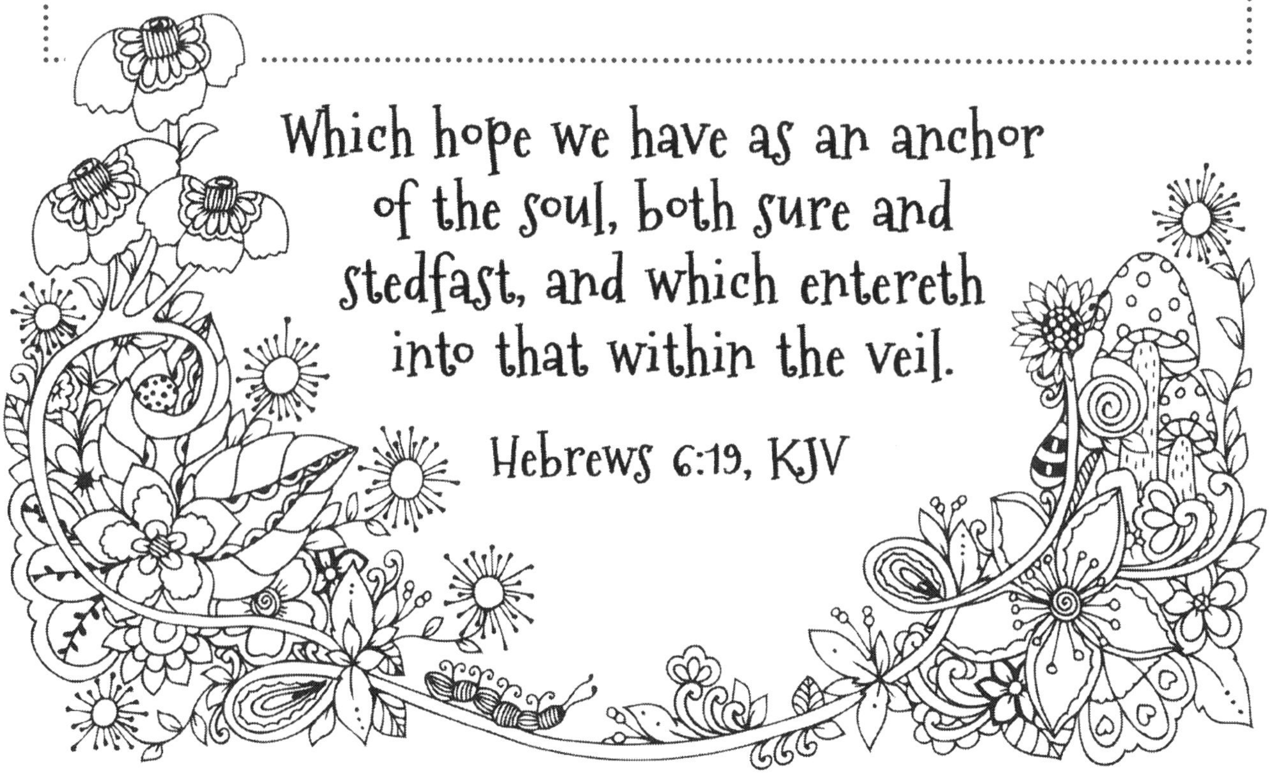

Which hope we have as an anchor of the soul, both sure and stedfast, and which entereth into that within the veil.

Hebrews 6:19, KJV

Notes

Let his faithful people rejoice in this honor and sing for joy on their beds. May the praise of God be in their mouths and a double-edged sword in their hands.
Psalm 149:5-6, NIV

Chapter 7

The Sword of the Spirit

When we look at The Sword of the Spirit in Ephesians Chapter 6, we discover that it's not the typical sword that comes to mind. At least not for me. My first thought would be your average 28-inch sword, but as we look a little closer at Paul's words, we see this isn't the case.

Swords come in all shapes and sizes, and the one that Paul is referring to in this context is an ancient weapon known as a machaira. A machaira is a smaller, double-edged sword that one could carry around with them at all times. In fact, the night that Jesus was arrested his followers asked Him if they should draw their swords. That's when Peter drew his machaira and cut off the ear of a soldier.

Hebrews 4:12 tells us, "For the word of God is alive and active. Sharper than any double-edged sword [machaira], it penetrates even to dividing soul and spirit, joints and marrow; it judges the thoughts and attitudes of the heart."

This metaphorical sword is something we could and should be carrying with us at all times. It's the word that we hide in our heart, and the truth that cuts deeper than any sword ever could.

Thayer's Lexicon defines the word this way, "The sword with which the Spirit subdues the impulses to sin and proves its own power and efficacy."

What Paul is telling us here is to arm ourselves with The Sword of the Spirit. He is telling us to prepare for battle by arming ourselves with the truth of God's Word. The reason truth is so vital to our protection is that Satan is the master of deception. He comes at us with half-truths.

He deceives by twisting God's Word, and he manipulates with tactics like shame, humiliation, and guilt. If we're not armed with the truth of God's Word, we're all the more likely to fall prey to his schemes.

DID YOU KNOW

The sword known as a machaira was used by Peter at the arrest of Jesus in the garden. It is said to have been named after Malchus the servant of the high priest whose ear was cut off by Peter.

One of the best examples of one wielding The Sword of the Spirit is found in Matthew Chapter 4 when Jesus was led into the wilderness to be tempted by the devil. After fasting for 40 days and 40 nights, He was faced with three temptations: hunger, pride, and power. Notice how these three temptations appeal to the body, the soul, and the spirit,

Materialism – To prioritize physical comforts over spiritual values

Egoism – Putting your interests above those of others and above those of God's

Hedonism – An elevated devotion to personal pleasure

DID YOU KNOW

The sword is "of the Spirit" because it is through the Holy Spirit that the truth is revealed to us in God's word. This is what Peter referred to as "epignosis", or the "deep knowledge" of God in 2 Peter 1:2.

Carry Your Sword

Satan attacks us by distracting our minds with the things of this world. His plan is to turn our minds away from the Lord and back onto ourselves. There isn't anything wrong with having material possessions and interests, nor is it bad to enjoy the pleasures that life has to offer. They do become sin however when we elevate the things of this world above the wisdom of God. And that's where Satan is crafty.

He knows the scriptures and will use them to tempt us. In fact, looking back at Matthew Chapter 4, we see that Satan used scripture as a tactic to tempt Jesus. Quoting Psalm 91:11 he says, "If thou be the Son of God, cast thyself down: for it is written, He shall give his angels charge concerning thee: and in their hands they shall bear thee up, lest at any time thou dash thy foot against a stone."

Charles Spurgeon writes, "Satan borrowed our Lord's weapon, and said, "It is written," but did not use the sword lawfully. It was not in the nature of the false fiend to quote correctly. He left out the necessary words, 'in all thy ways': thus, he made the promise say what in truth it never suggested."

Jesus was able to wield the sword, because he knew the Word of God. He rightly divided the truth in a way only those who know the Word of God can.

2 Timothy 2:15 reads, "Study to shew thyself approved unto God, a workman that needeth not to be ashamed, rightly dividing the word of truth." (KJV)

When the Word of God is firmly planted in our hearts we can use it in our defence. We can discern that which is good and that which is evil. We can see the wolf coming before we're devoured.

When we study the word of God and memorize the scripture we are arming ourselves for the battle. When we truly know the scripture, we can discern when it's being manipulated or when it's being used for God's glory.

Here's an important thing to remember when it comes to your armor. A sword is useless if you don't carry it with you. If you don't study God's Word, it won't come to mind when you're in need of a sword. If you're not reading the Bible and learning God's Word, you'll be easily swayed by half truths. The Bible warns us about wolves in sheep's clothing—the preachers who are more interested in their savings account than they are in saving your soul. Churches that are more concerned in filling the pews than they are with filling the kingdom of heaven. They will tickle your ears with false doctrine and lead people astray. But when you are in the Word and you know the Word, you can wisely discern right from wrong.

DID YOU KNOW

The sword wielded by the devil in the wilderness was not the sword of the Spirit, but rather an inferior sword of deception.

And finally, remember to hold that sword firmly. A sword can't be affective if you're holding it loosely. In Psalm 119 David talks about how the commandments made him wiser than his enemies, and how he was able to adhere to God's Word because he loved God's Word. He meditated on the Word that was firmly planted in his heart.

O how love I thy law! it is my meditation all the day. Thou through thy commandments hast made me wiser than mine enemies: for they are ever with me. (Psalm 119:97-98, NIV)

Q. What advantage do we have when we are in the Word, and know the Word of God?

____

____

____

____

Q. What are some of the tactics that Satan uses against us?

Q. What disadvantage is there to not studying God's Word regularly?

The raw recruit is not trusted
with the general's sword; but here are you
armed with the weapon of God the Holy
Ghost, and called upon to bear that sacred
sword which is so gloriously wielded
by the Lord God himself.
- C. H. Spurgeon -

Q. How was David made wiser than his enemies?

Q. What are some examples of "wolves in sheep's clothing?"

Notes

Answer Key

Chapter 1

Q. According to a survey conducted by the Barna Group, what percentage of people who refer to themselves as "Christian" believe Satan is just a symbol of evil, and not a living being?

A. 40%

Q. Which two realms are mentioned in this chapter?

A. The physical realm and the spiritual realm.

Q. What does Revelation 12:4 say? Write the verse out here:

A. Its tail swept a third of the stars out of the sky and flung them to the earth. The dragon stood in front of the woman who was about to give birth, so that it might devour her child the moment he was born. (NIV)

Q. What does Satan masquerade as?

A. An angel of light.

Q. Who is known as The Ruler of This World?

A. Satan

Q. What does James 4:7 teach us about handling temptation?

A. It tells us to submit ourselves to God. To resist temptation and Satan will flee from us.

Q. Peter warns us about the dangers of Satan, but then reveals to us how we are to overcome him. What is Peter's advice to us?

A. Resist him. Stand firm in the faith.

Q. What are the different names given or used to describe Satan in the Bible?

Job 1:6 - Satan
Isaiah 14:12 – Morning Star
Ezekiel 28:14 - Guardian Cherub
Matthew 4:1 – The Devil
Matthew 4:3 – The Tempter
Matthew 9:34 – Prince of Demons
Matthew 12:24 - Beelzebul
Matthew 13:19 – The Evil One
John 14:30 – Prince of This World
2 Corinthians 4:4 – The God of This Age
2 Corinthians 6:15 - Belial
Ephesians 2:2 – The Ruler of the Kingdom of the Air
Revelation 9:11 - Apollyon
Revelation 12:9 – The Great Dragon, The Ancient Serpent, The Devil, and Satan
Revelation 12:10 – The Accuser of Our Brothers and Sisters

Chapter 2

Q. What is the meaning of "Sine Cera?"

A. The words mean "without wax." The words "Sine Cera" represented honest and sincere merchants.

Q. According to the writer of the book of Hebrews, what are we to run with?

A. We are to run the race with perseverance.

Q. What is the meaning of the phrase "gird your loins?"

A. It means prepare yourself for battle. This was done by a soldier lifting up his tunic and tucking it into his belt so that he could move freely and swiftly on the battlefield.

Q. Where did the Holy Spirit lead Jesus to be tempted? In what 3 ways was Jesus tempted?

A. The desert.

Q. If we want to live in fullness of life, abounding with joy, what must we protect?

A. Our hearts and our minds. We need to fight for our families, our faith, our marriages, and in fact, we need to fight for our joy.

Q. According to Hebrews 12:1, what is it that can so easily entangle us?
And so, what are we to do?

A. Sin. We are to throw off everything that hinders including the sin that so easily entangles.

Q. When does a person's integrity become hypocrisy?

A. When we don't practice in secret what we hold dear in the light.

Chapter 3

Q. What are Paul's words in 2 Corinthians 10:5 likened to?

A. Warfare.

Q. What were Roman breastplates made of?

A. They were generally made of leather, bronze, or iron.

Q. What does it mean to put on The Breastplate of Righteousness?

A. To put on The Breastplate of Righteousness is to live a righteous life. It's something we put on every day.

Q. What does Proverbs 4:23 tell us to guard? Write the verse out here.

A. It says to guard your heart, for everything you do flows from it.

Above all else, guard your heart, for everything you do flows from it. (Proverbs 4:23, NIV)

Q. What are some practical ways you can protect your heart?

A. This answer will be different for everyone as we see the changes we need to make in our lives.

Fill in the Blanks:

If you know that he is ________________, you know that everyone who does ________________ has been born of him. (1 John 2:29, NIV)

A. righteous, what is right

For with the heart man believeth unto _________________; and with the mouth confession is made _________________. (Romans 10:10, KJV)

A. righteousness, unto salvation

All Scripture is God-breathed and is useful for teaching, rebuking, correcting and _____________________________, so that the servant of God may be thoroughly _______________ for every good work.
(2 Timothy 3:16-17, NIV)

training in righteousness, equipped

Q. With what are we to fill our minds?

A. The truth of God's Word.

Q. What does Paul say we should take captive? How do we do that?

A. He says we should take our thoughts captive. We demolish arguments and every pretension that sets itself up against the knowledge of God. We make our thoughts obedience to Christ.

Q. What are some reoccurring thoughts that you struggle to take captive? What are some enticing lies that Satan has told you about these thoughts? What are some truths that can tear these lies down?

A. These answers will be different for everyone.

Chapter 4

Q. What were the sandals Roman soldiers wore made of?

A. Caligae were heavy-duty leather sandals with hobnailed soles. The hobnails were hammered into the soles of the sandals to offer the soldiers extra grip much like the modern-day cleats worn by football players

Q. Who were singing hymns and praying in prison in the middle of the night?

A. Paul and Silas

Q. How do we rebuke Satan's lies?

A. With the truth of God's Word.

Q. List some of the trials you have experienced in your life. After each one, mark down whether you think you were strengthened or defeated by it:

A. This answer is personal and will be different for everyone.

Q. What outweighs our momentary affliction?

Faith tells us that that eternal glory outweighs our momentary affliction by far. It reminds us that we have a home beyond the scope of this world, and points us straight to the salvation of God.

Q. What does God promise to those who wait upon the Lord?

A. They shall renew their strength; they shall mount up with wings as eagles; they shall run, and not be weary; and they shall walk, and not faint. (Isaiah 40:31)

Q. How did Josephus describe the soles of the Roman soldiers' shoes?

A. Full of thick and sharp nails.

Fill in the Blanks:

Therefore, my dear brothers and sisters, ________________. Let nothing move you. Always give yourselves fully to the work of the Lord, because you know that your labor in the Lord is not ____________________.

(1 Corinthians 15:58, NIV)

A. Stand firm, in vain

Q. How do we stand firm in our faith?

A. Don't waiver when you're tested and tried. Don't run when you're standing alone. Don't give up when the going is tough.

Q. When was the last time you let Satan steal your joy? What happened? How should you have reacted instead?

A. These two are personal answers and will be different for everyone.

Chapter 5

Q. What are the fiery darts spoken of in Ephesians Chapter 6?

A. They are lust. The less we are satisfied, the more we'll be tempted. And so, we lust after power, money, attention, love, food, sex, beauty, and more. Satan knows that dissatisfaction is the Achilles' heel of mankind. He knows that we hunger for more and so we're met with temptation day after day.

Q. How are the shields made fire-proof?

A. They were immersed in water.

Q. From where does faith originate?

A. Faith comes by hearing and hearing by the word of God.

Q. Why is dissatisfaction so dangerous to a believer?

A. Because the less satisfied we are, the more we'll be tempted. Satan knows that dissatisfaction is the Achilles' heel of mankind. He knows that we hunger for more and so we're met with temptation day after day.

Q. What are the faith-building blocks we glean from God's word?

A. Joy, peace, love, and hope.

Q. What has cleansing power?

A. God's Word.

Fill in the Blanks:

No ____________________ that is formed against thee shall prosper; and every tongue that shall rise against thee in judgment thou shalt condemn. This is the heritage of the servants of the Lord, and their ___________________ is of me, saith the Lord. (Isaiah 54:17, KJV)

A. Weapon, righteousness

Be ________________ and _____________________. Do not be afraid or terrified because of them, for the Lord your God goes with you; he will never leave you nor forsake you." (Deuteronomy 31:6, NIV)

A. strong, courageous

But you, Lord, are _______________________ around me, my glory, the One who lifts my head high. (Psalm 3:3, NIV)

A. A shield

Q. What are some of the lies that Satan has been firing at you? Under each one, mark down a fire-quenching truth.

A. This answer is personal and would be different for everyone.

Chapter 6

Q. What are some long-term goals that you've had? What are some of the short-term benefits that either slowed you down or presented them from happening?

A. This answer is personal and would be different for everyone.

Fill in the Blanks:

For in this hope we ________________________. But hope that is seen is no hope at all. Who hopes for what they already have? But if we hope for what we do not ________________________, we wait for it ____________________________. (Romans 8:24-25, NIV)

A. were saved, yet have, patiently

If only for this life we have ________________ in Christ, we are of all people most to be ___________________. (1 Corinthians 15:19, NIV)

A. hope, pitied

In his great mercy he has given us new birth into a __________________ __________________ through the resurrection of Jesus Christ from the dead. (1 Peter 1:3b, NIV)

A. living hope

Q. What two things are the temporary shelters found in Leviticus 23:42-43 a physical reminder of?

A. They are a physical reminder to them of what their ancestors had to live in for over 40 years as they wandered through the desert on their way to the promised land. It's also a physical reminder to us that this world is nothing more than a temporary dwelling as we wait for the return of our Lord.

Q. What is The Helmet of Salvation according to 1 Thessalonians 5:8?

A. The Hope of Salvation

Q. What happened on the mountain in Matthew Chapter 17? Who was there with Jesus?

A. Jesus transfigured before them. His face shone like the sun, and his clothes became as white as the light.

Moses and Elijah were with Him.

Q. What did Moses and Elijah each represent at the transfiguration? What connection would this have to The Helmet of Salvation?

A. Moses represented believers who enter the kingdom through death. Elijah, a prophet who never saw death but was taken up to heaven in a whirlwind, represents believers who enter the kingdom through the rapture of the church.

Chapter 7

Q. What advantage do we have when we are in the word, and know the word of God?

A. When we truly know the scripture, we can discern when it's being manipulated or when it's being used for God's glory.

Q. What are some of the tactics that Satan uses against us?

A. He manipulates with tactics like shame, humiliation, and guilt.

Q. What disadvantage is there to not studying God's word regularly?

A. If you don't study God's Word, it won't come to mind when you're in need of a sword. If you're not reading the Bible and learning God's Word, you'll be easily swayed by half truths.

Q. How was David made wiser than his enemies?

A. The commandments made him wiser than his enemies because he loved and adhered to God's Word.

Q. What are some examples of "wolves in sheep's clothing?"

A. Preachers or churches who are more interested in money than the truth of God's Word.

Made in the USA
Monee, IL
30 July 2020

37266819R00051